Growing Up Corporate:

Mastering the Intern Sprint Survival Guide

Dr. Deborah Stubblefield

DOD Publications

Growing Up Corporate:
Mastering the Intern Sprint Survival Guide
by Dr. Deborah Stubblefield

Published by DOD Publications

ISBN: 978-1-967603-03-9 (paperback)

Printed in the United States of America.

DEDICATION

Dedicated to all those who supported, guided, and encouraged me along the way—those who helped me reach the starting line of Corporate America and empowered me to navigate its challenges. Your belief in me has been an enduring gift, and for that, I am deeply grateful.

CONTENTS

☀ Wisdom Moment

"Know ye not that they which run in a race run all, but one receiveth the prize? So run, that ye may obtain."
1 Corinthians 9:24 (KJV)

Introduction

Welcome to your Survival Guide, which is a turbo-charged playbook for Millennials, Gen Z, and Gen Alpha to sprint through any internship, packed with checklists and plug-and-play templates. So, let's begin…

🌞 The Spark: From Status Symbol to Real Work

- **Dream vs. Reality:** Like you, I craved that first summer job – for status, skill-building, and independence. Yet every fast-food and retail application felt like a closed door.

- **Unexpected Break:** Near a high-school semester's end, my grandmother's friend called: her granddaughter could not take an internship, and she asked, would I? Grandma said, "Yes!" ✅

- **Mindset Shift**: I went from "just wanting to make money" to realizing that this opportunity could launch skills and confidence I never knew I needed.

This survival guide is not just a book of theory; it is your career blueprint. In four power-packed chapters you will master SMART goals, nail Day 1, run with Ten Powerful "Be's," and finish strong. Many interns and professionals have found these suggestions helpful and widely used them. Ready? Lace up and let's go!

How to Use This Guide

★ Reflect on the 📖 **Wisdom Moments** and 🔶 **Action Responses**.

★ Read each chapter overview first.

★ Follow ✔ **Quick Wins** and 💡 **Key Actions**.

★ Apply templates from **Resources** for instant impact.

📖 Wisdom Moment

"If any of you lack wisdom, let him ask of God, that giveth to all men liberally… and it shall be given him."
James 1:5 (KJV)

🔸 Action Response

• List two areas where you feel least prepared (e.g., industry jargon, software).
• Schedule 15-minute "Wisdom Chats" with a mentor this week.
• Start a "Wisdom Log," note one new tip or insight daily.

A "Wisdom Chat" is a wonderful way to intentionally spend time gaining insight from your mentor. Your time with your mentor should be purposeful, meaning schedule 20 – 45 minutes and have an agenda (e.g., topic, questions, follow-up items). Then journal the wisdom that you received on your "Wisdom Log," which can be done on your phone or in a physical journal.

Chapter 1: On Your Mark

Every internship journey starts with a single step: getting into the race. Like the marathons I participated in with the U.S. Air Force community, with their courses weaving through flat stretches, hills, and curves, an internship feels brief yet demands endurance.

▓ **Internships** may span just 6 - 10 weeks, but like a marathon, they demand steady pacing and preparation. **Your goal? Start confidently, stay focused, pace yourself well, and finish strong!**

How to Use This Chapter

- ✔ Plan Your Path.
- ✔ Draft two SMART goals.
- ✔ Complete the **Pre-Internship Check**.
- ✔ Perfect your "Why I Want This" pitch.

✨ Pre-Race Prep

Imagine, if you were cooking or competitively running, before you turn on the stove or step onto the track, you gather ingredients or stretch your muscles. Preparing for an internship follows the same rule.

1. Plan Your Path ✅

- **For whom do you want to work?**
- **What skills or experiences matter most?**
- **When (spring, summer, fall) and where (in-state or out-of-state)?**

Answering these narrows your search and sharpens your pitch at career fairs and on applications.

2. Set SMART Goals 📖

- **Specific:** *Choose one skill or project to master.*
- **Measurable:** *Define weekly check-ins.*
- **Achievable:** *Allocate realistic hours.*
- **Relevant:** *Align with your career vision.*
- **Time-bound:** *Set a clear finish date.*

Example: By June 30, I will lead one team presentation to boost my public-speaking confidence.

3. Find Opportunities 💡

- **Scan company websites, job boards, career fairs, LinkedIn, and campus career centers.**

Caution: Be careful answering unsolicited opportunities and sharing information online. Verify that requests originate from company representatives using official business emails.

- **Research each firm's mission, products, and culture** to learn three facts about each employer.

- **Prepare three unique talking points for recruiters** to help craft your 30-second intro (*see the Resources chapter*).

🔍 Pre-Internship Check

Rate yourself 1 - 5 (1=Strongly Disagree; 5=Strongly Agree) in the following six areas by circling the appropriate number for your response.

Section 1 – Communication & Teamwork

1. I write clear emails and reports. [1 2 3 4 5]
2. I ask questions when I am unsure. [1 2 3 4 5]
3. I listen fully before responding. [1 2 3 4 5]
4. I collaborate smoothly on group tasks. [1 2 3 4 5]

Section 2 – Professional Attitude
5. I value punctuality and reliability. [1 2 3 4 5]
6. I know how to seek help if I get stuck. [1 2 3 4 5]
7. I respect rules and procedures. [1 2 3 4 5]
8. I adapt my behavior for formal settings. [1 2 3 4 5]

Section 3 – Time Management
9. I plan my schedule to meet deadlines. [1 2 3 4 5]
10. I use calendars/reminders effectively. [1 2 3 4 5]
11. I break big tasks into steps. [1 2 3 4 5]
12. I ask for support if overwhelmed. [1 2 3 4 5]

Section 4 – Initiative & Problem-Solving
13. I volunteer for extra roles. [1 2 3 4 5]
14. I brainstorm solutions before asking for help. [1 2 3 4 5]
15. I clarify expectations when unclear. [1 2 3 4 5]
16. I reflect on mistakes and adjust. [1 2 3 4 5]

Section 5 – Digital Literacy
17. I email professionally and promptly. [1 2 3 4 5]
18. I navigate Word, Excel, and PowerPoint well. [1 2 3 4 5]
19. I practice strong online security habits. [1 2 3 4 5]
20. I vet sources for research reliability. [1 2 3 4 5]

Section 6 – Career Clarity & Confidence
21. I can name two skills I want to grow. [1 2 3 4 5]
22. I have researched internships in my field. [1 2 3 4 5]
23. I can articulate my internship goals. [1 2 3 4 5]
24. I feel ready to introduce myself to professionals. [1 2 3 4 5]

Total your score (max 120) to spot strengths and your pre-race growth areas. **Use your results then to focus on practicing, setting mini-goals, and building confidence before Day 1.**

✔ **Quick Win:** Any score ≤ 3? Set a mini-SMART goal now.

🚀 The Starting Line

Your first day is more than orientation, it is your launch pad. Emotions swirl: excitement, adrenaline, nerves, or a flicker of fear. ✅ Combat anxiety with:

- Build a support circle. Share your hopes and nerves with family, mentors, or a therapist.
- Create a routine. Schedule meals, focus blocks, and breaks to anchor your days.
- Use affirmations. Speak positive truths aloud: *"I am prepared, I will learn, I will excel."*

Take one step at a time and take a deep breath. You are ready to run your race.

🗒 Chapter 1 Action Plan

[ ] Ask two targeted questions about industry terms by the end of the week.

[ ] Schedule one "Wisdom Chat" with a mentor.

[ ] Journal: Log a daily Wisdom insight for one week.

Notes

Notes

💡 Wisdom Moment

"The ants are a people not strong, yet they prepare their meat in the summer."
Proverbs 30:25 (KJV)

📌 Action Response

- One week pre-start, gather your gear: attire, tech, and commute plan.
- Do a dry-run commute and mock presentation.
- Define your personal "prize." Write one clear outcome you will achieve during your internship (e.g., lead a project, secure a return offer).
- Create a "Go-Bag" folder with policies, org chart, and your SMART goals.

Chapter 2: Get Set, Go!

The starter's pistol has fired…**you are on Day 1** 🟢 of your internship. That first step can stir excitement and nerves in equal measure. You will not sprint the whole course; instead, settle into a steady pace that keeps you alert, resourceful, and focused on your finish line because too fast leads to burnout, too slow invites complacency.

How to Use This Chapter

✔ Bookmark the **Three Ps** on Day 1.

✔ Review ⚠️ **Common Pitfalls**.

✔ Review 😖 **Common Frustrations**.

✔ Learn 🐘 **"The Elephant"** strategy.

✔ Capture your **Intern Launch** on Week 1.

▦ Launch Day Essentials

1. **Punctuality**
   ✔ Arrive 5 minutes early.
   ✔ Alert your supervisor if you will be late promptly.

2. **Performance**
   ✔ Organize tasks with clear milestones & due dates.
   ✔ Send weekly updates:

   > *3 achievements • 2 roadblocks • 1 next step*

3. **Professionalism**
   ✔ Match your attire to company culture.
   ✔ Use clear, courteous language.

⚠️ Common Mistakes

1. **Procrastination:** Shrinks your timeline and spikes stress → *Plan backward from deadlines.*
2. **Sloppy Communication:** Save emojis and slang for friends, not your boss → Draft → Proofread.
3. **Etiquette Missteps:** Guard phone use, badge in properly, and follow "break time" rules → Learn "break time" & device rules.

😣 Common Frustrations

1. **Project Assignments:** *Tasks shift.* Embrace flexibility and embrace learning on the fly.
2. **Impostor Syndrome:** Counter self-doubt with SMART goals and daily journaling.
3. **Ambiguity:** Use a simple Plan-Do-Check-Act or DMAIC cycle to break down uncertainty.
4. **Limited Offers:** Not every intern is hired for a return internship or a full-time role. Focus on your performance, not just the outcome.

🐘 The Elephant in the Room

Unfortunately, everyone has biases, but some coworkers specifically have low expectations of interns. These coworkers may greet interns with skepticism or stereotypes. 📖 You cannot change or control their mindset, but you can control your actions (it's a choice) by:

- Showing respect for institutional knowledge.
- Staying humble and curious about what you do not know.
- Allowing your work to dismantle assumptions one deliverable at a time, delivering consistent, quality work.

▢ Chapter 2 Action Plan

[ ] Do your dry run commute this week.

[ ] Set a calendar reminder: weekly status update.

[ ] Identify one break time etiquette question and ask your supervisor or Human Resources (also called HR).

✎ Intern Launch

This section is your internship week one companion. Take 5-7 minutes three times a day to journal the first 5-day journey of your internship.

My Daily *Launch Check-In*	Day 1 Date: _____
Morning Check-In ***Stress & Energy*** (*1 is low – 5 is high*): • Rate your stress level: _____ • Rate today's energy level: _____ ***Morning Intent*** • Today's Gratitude Affirmation: "*I give thanks in all things.*" (*Reference: 1 Thessalonians 5:18*) ***Workday Info:*** *Start Time: _____ End Time: _____* **Midday Micro-Break Pause** ***Goal Chunking:*** • Write one SMART goal for the week. • List two small steps you will take each day. • At week's end, note progress and one area for grace.	**End-of-Day Reflection** • Today, I am grateful for ... . • A strength (e.g., brave, kind) I used today was… . . . . • Say a short prayer, "Thank you, Lord, for this strength."

My Daily	Day 2

My Daily
Launch Check-In

Day 2

Date: _____

Morning Check-In
Stress & Energy (*1 is low – 5 is high*):

- Rate your stress level: _____
- Rate today's energy level: _____

Morning Intent

- Today's Focus Affirmation:
  "Be still and know that I am God."
  (*Reference: Psalms 46:10*)

. . . .
. . . .

Today's Focus:
Set your own focus areas:

. . . .
. . . .
. . . .
. . . .
. . . .
. . . .
. . . .
. . . .

Midday Micro-Break Pause
Breath-Centered Mindfulness

- Close eyes.
- Inhale for 4 counts.
- Hold 2 counts.
- Exhale 6 counts.
- Repeat for 3 minutes and note effect.

. . . .
. . . .
. . . .
. . . .
. . . .

End-of-Day Reflection

- I am grateful for *(name 3 things)* …

. . . .
. . . .
. . . .
. . . .
. . . .
. . . .
. . . .
. . . .
. . . .

- Challenges I faced *(1-2 challenges)* …

. . . .
. . . .
. . . .
. . . .
. . . .
. . . .
. . . .
. . . .

- Tomorrow's focus…

. . . .
. . . .
. . . .
. . . .
. . . .
. . . .
. . . .
. . . .

My Daily	**Day 3**
Launch Check-In	Date: _____

Morning Check-In
Stress & Energy (*1 is low – 5 is high*):

- Rate your stress level: _____
- Rate today's energy level: _____

Morning Intent

- Today's Growth Affirmation:
  "*My thoughts & behaviors conform to God's standard.*"
  (*Reference: Romans 12:1-2*)

. . . .
. . . .

Today's Focus:
Set your own focus areas:

. . . .
. . . .
. . . .
. . . .
. . . .
. . . .
. . . .
. . . .

Midday Micro-Break Pause
Cognitive Reframing:

- Note a negative thought.
- Ask: "Is this 100% true?"
- Write a balanced alternative.
- Repeat aloud with conviction.

. . . .
. . . .
. . . .
. . . .
. . . .

End-of-Day Reflection

- I am grateful for…

. . . .
. . . .
. . . .
. . . .
. . . .
. . . .
. . . .
. . . .
. . . .

- Challenges I faced…

. . . .
. . . .
. . . .
. . . .
. . . .
. . . .
. . . .
. . . .
. . . .

- Tomorrow's focus…

. . . .
. . . .
. . . .
. . . .
. . . .
. . . .
. . . .
. . . .
. . . .

My Daily	Day 4
Launch Check-In	Date: _____

Morning Check-In
Stress & Energy (*1 is low – 5 is high*):

- Rate your stress level: _____
- Rate today's energy level: _____

Morning Intent

- Today's Self-Kindness Affirmation: "*God's steadfast mercy is new towards me every morning.*" (*Reference: Lamentations 3:22–23*)

. . . .
. . . .

Midday Micro-Break Pause
Three-Step Self-Compassion Break:

- Write one sentence naming your pain ("I feel…").
- Write, "Everyone feels this way, and I am not alone."
- Write a kind phrase to yourself ("May I be gentle…").
- Read Lamentations 3:22 and pause to feel God's mercy.

. . . .
. . . .
. . . .
. . . .
. . . .
.. . .
.. . .
. . . .
. . . .
. . . .
. . . .

End-of-Day Reflection

- I am grateful for…

. . . .
. . . .
. . . .
. . . .
. . . .
. . . .
. . . .
. . . .
. . . .

- Challenges I faced…

. . . .
. . . .
. . . .
. . . .
. . . .
. . . .
. . . .
. . . .
. . . .

- Tomorrow's focus…

. . . .
. . . .
. . . .
. . . .
. . . .
. . . .
. . . .
. . . .
. . . .

My Daily	Day 5
Launch Check-In	Date: _____

Morning Check-In

Stress & Energy (*1 is low – 5 is high*):

- Rate your stress level: _____
- Rate today's energy level: _____

Morning Intent

- Today's Grace Affirmation:
  "God's grace (mercy & lovingkindness) is sufficient."
  (*Reference: 2 Corinthians 12:9*)

. . . .
. . . .

Midday Micro-Break Pause

Goal Progress Monitoring & Planning:

- Revisit your SMART goal & tasks; check your plan – *are you on track?*
- Meditate on 2 Corinthians 12:9: *"My grace is sufficient."*
- Adjust your mini tasks; and celebrate those completed.
- Set a SMART goal for next week.

. . . .
. . . .
. . . .
. . . .
. . . .
. . . .
. . . .
. . . .
. . . .
. . . .
. . . .
. . . .

End-of-Day Reflection

- I am grateful for...

. . . .
. . . .
. . . .
. . . .
. . . .
. . . .
. . . .
. . . .
. . . .

- Challenges I faced...

. . . .
. . . .
. . . .
. . . .
. . . .
. . . .
. . . .
. . . .

- Lessons I learned...

. . . .
. . . .
. . . .
. . . .
. . . .
. . . .
. . . .
. . . .

🚀 Wisdom Moment

"I returned, and saw under the sun, that the race is not to the swift… but time and chance happeneth them all."
Ecclesiastes 9:11 (KJV)

🚩 Action Response

- Carve out 30 minutes daily for your top project.
- Block 1-hour weekly buffer for urgent tasks.
- Reflect each Friday: what fell through the cracks? Adjust next week's buffer.

Chapter 3: Run & Finish Strong

Weeks into your internship, every assignment, conversation, and choice shapes your final evaluation.

🏃 Mid-Race Checkpoint

You are now weeks into your internship, every assignment, conversation, and choice shapes your final evaluation. Your consistency and adaptability define your legacy. Treat the entire term as one continuous interview: leaders, peers, and mentors are watching your consistency, resilience, and growth from start to finish.

🔄 Race Dynamics

- Peer Competition: You and fellow interns share goals, and a limited number of future spots.
- Sponsor Relationships: Schedule check-ins, ask for feedback, and share small wins.

How to Use This Chapter

- ✔ Treat every task as a **Continuous Interview**.
- ✔ Practice one "Be" daily (**Ten Powerful "Be's"**).
- ✔ Build your **Next-Step Network**.

🔄 Continuous Interview

- Every email and meeting counts.
- Schedule mid-internship check-ins.
- Ask: "What's one thing I can improve?"

☀️ Stand-Out Behaviors: Ten Powerful "Be's"

1. Be **Proactive** *& Action-Oriented* ✅

2. Be **Professional** *in Dress & Demeanor* 📖

3. Be **Curious**: *ask great questions* 💡

4. Be **Relational**: *grow your network* 🤝

5. Be **Ethical**: *honor policies* ⚖️

6. Be **Clear** *& Effective* 📝

7. Be **Accountable**: *own mistakes & solutions* ✔️

8. Be **Open to Feedback**: *listen & iterate* 🔄

9. Be **Adaptable**: *pivot with grace* 🌿

10. Be a **Leader**: *step up on tasks* 🦁

Each "Be" is a choice. Choose each "Be" deliberately. These behaviors will set you apart and position you for success.

💡 **Key Action:** Journal your weekly "Be" progress.

📋 Chapter 3 Action Plan

[ ] Schedule a mid-internship check-in with your manager

[ ] Journal one "Be" you practiced each day

[ ] Draft your Next-Step Networking email.

Notes

Notes

▓ Wisdom Moment

"Man goeth forth unto his work and to his labour until the evening."
Psalms 104:23 (KJV)

◆ Action Response

- Time-block: Focus Work | Collaboration | Learning.
- Each afternoon, list today's top 3 wins, and tomorrow's top 3 tasks.
- Set an evening cutoff; no work after 7 PM to recharge.

Chapter 4: The Cool Down

You have crossed the finish line. Now it is time to reflect, give thanks, and plan your next leg.

❄ You have done the work, built the skills, and faced every challenge. Now pause, reflect, give thanks, and chart your next steps.

How to Use This Chapter
✔ Execute **Wrap-Up Courtesies**.
✔ Reflect with the **Post-Internship Check**.
✔ Kickstart your **Next Steps Blueprint**.

🙌 Wrap-Up Courtesies
✔ Send a brief thank-you email on your last day (BCC your team). (*See the Resources chapter*).
✔ Connect on LinkedIn.
✔ If you return to campus, visit the career fair table next semester.

📝 Post-Internship Check
Rate yourself 1 – 5 (1=Strongly Disagree; 5=Strongly Agree), by circling the appropriate number for your response. Compare scores to your pre-internship questionnaire to measure growth and set new SMART goals.

Section 1 – Communication & Collaboration
1. I kept supervisors updated and welcomed feedback. [1 2 3 4 5]
2. I spoke up in meetings with ideas or questions. [1 2 3 4 5]
3. I listened actively and paraphrased others' points. [1 2 3 4 5]
4. I worked constructively with teammates. [1 2 3 4 5]

Section 2 – Professionalism & Work Ethic

5. I arrived early and stayed engaged in meetings. [1 2 3 4 5]

6. I adapted my attire and conduct to fit the culture. [1 2 3 4 5]

7. I used feedback to improve my work. [1 2 3 4 5]

8. I always respected confidentiality. [1 2 3 4 5]

Section 3 – Time Management & Productivity

9. I met deadlines without last-minute rushes. [1 2 3 4 5]

10. I tracked tasks with calendars or tools. [1 2 3 4 5]

11. I alerted my supervisor when faced with delays. [1 2 3 4 5]

12. I balanced internship duties with other commitments. [1 2 3 4 5]

Section 4 – Initiative & Problem-Solving

13. I volunteered for extra challenges. [1 2 3 4 5]

14. I proposed multiple solutions when stuck. [1 2 3 4 5]

15. I asked targeted questions to clarify tasks. [1 2 3 4 5]

16. I reflected on setbacks and adapted. [1 2 3 4 5]

Section 5 – Digital & Technical Application

17. I learned new tools to boost efficiency. [1 2 3 4 5]

18. I communicated professionally online. [1 2 3 4 5]

19. I mastered basic functions of unfamiliar systems. [1 2 3 4 5]

20. I documented processes to aid future interns. [1 2 3 4 5]

Section 6 – Career Growth & Next Steps

21. I can list three skills I developed. [1 2 3 4 5]

22. I have a clear plan for ongoing growth. [1 2 3 4 5]

23. I feel confident sharing accomplishments. [1 2 3 4 5]

24. I have set new SMART goals for my career. [1 2 3 4 5]

Total Score (out of 120): _____

Use your score to pinpoint strengths and areas to develop before your next race.

✳ Next Steps Blueprint

1. **Résumé Refresh:** Highlight three concrete wins.

2. **Goal Reset:** Write two new SMART goals based on your lowest self-assessment areas.

3. **Stay Connected:** Schedule quarterly check-ins with mentors and/or colleagues.

Your race never truly ends. Each goal achieved is a step towards your next victory.

▢ Chapter 4 Action Plan

[ ] Send your on-point thank-you (see the Resources chapter).

[ ] Choose two new goals and put them on your calendar.

[ ] Set LinkedIn or another calendar reminder: check in with mentors.

Notes

Notes

Internship Reflection

Use these reflection prompts to deepen your insights and fuel your next leap:

1. What surprised me most about my internship/role and why?

_____

2. Which mistake taught me the biggest lesson?

_____

3. How did I practice each of the Ten Powerful "Be's"?

4. When did I feel most like an impostor, and what changed it?

5. Which "elephant in the room" moment did I navigate best? Or least?

6. How did my SMART goals drive my daily focus?

7. What skill would I rate a 5/5 now, and what is next to master?

8. Which relationship or conversation will I nurture going forward?

Notes

Notes

Resources

📋 Plug-and-Play Templates for Instant Impact

1. **On-Point Thank-You Email**
    Subject: Thank You!
    Hello All,

    Thank you for supporting and/or mentoring me during my summer internship at [Company].

    Your support and feedback on [Project/Task] sharpened my skills in [Skill]. I appreciate you taking the time to [specific support].

    Looking forward to staying connected and applying these lessons in my next role.

    Warm regards,
    [Your Name]
    [Email] | [Phone] | [LinkedIn URL]

2. **30-Second Intro (Elevator Speech)**
    Hi, I am [Name], a [Your Major/Role] at [School/Organization]. I am passionate about [Industry/Skill], especially how [Company] turns [Key Product/Service] into [Key Benefit]. I would love to discuss how my [Relevant Experience] can support your team's next big project.

💡 **Key Action:** Feel free to use an AI tool to craft clear professional communications. Be sure to assign the AI tool a role and give it a clear prompt command to achieve the expected outcome.

3. Sample SMART Goals

Goal 1: By August 1, I will complete three research briefs on [Topic] and present findings to my supervisor to strengthen my analytical skills.

Build your SMART GOALS
Specific: What do you want to do and why?
Measurable: How will you know when you meet the goal?
Achievable: How will you achieve this goal?
Realistic: Does it make sense to achieve this goal now?
Timebound: When do you want to achieve this goal?

Goal 2: By July 15, I will lead one cross-departmental meeting to practice facilitation and stakeholder communication.

Build your SMART GOALS
Specific: What do you want to do and why?
Measurable: How will you know when you meet the goal?
Achievable: How will you achieve this goal?
Realistic: Does it make sense to achieve this goal now?
Timebound: When do you want to achieve this goal?

4. End of Internship – Out of Office Email
Subject: Out of Office/End of Internship

Hello,

Thank you for contacting me. However, as of [enter the date], my internship has concluded. For continued support and information regarding my work scope and/or specific projects, please reach out to [Supervisor's Name or name of person who inherited the work].

Thank you,

[Your Name]

🔲 Glossary Highlights (See full guide for 90+ terms)

Name	Acronym/Definition
Conflict Management	Definition: Methods for handling disagreements, preferably in a way that resolves conflict in a way that arrives at an agreement. Example: When two interns argue over who writes the report, you guide them to list each person's tasks and agree on a split.
Critical Thinking	Definition: Examining facts carefully to make smart decisions or solve problem solve. Example: You compare two sales reports and pick the one with more reliable data.
Integrity	Definition: Doing what is right even when no one is watching. Example: You admit a data entry error and fix it without being asked.
Mentor	Definition: An experienced person who guides and supports your growth. Example: Your mentor reads your draft presentation and gives tips on improving it.
PDCA (Plan-Do-Check-Act)	Definition: A four-step cycle – plan, do, check, act – used to improve processes over time. Example: You plan a new method for a task, try it for a week (do), review if it saved time (check), then adjust your process (act).

Name	Acronym/Definition
Performance	Definition: The completion of a task and the level at which you met the company's/your supervisor's expectations while doing it. Example: You finish every assignment on time (as defined by your supervisor) and with few mistakes; impressive performance.
Six Sigma Methodology	Definition: A data-driven process that aims to reduce errors and improve quality in work. Example: You track how many worksheets arrive with mistakes, use the data to find the main causes, and update training to reduce errors.
Skills	Definition: Abilities you develop through practice, like writing, speaking, or coding. Example: Your data-entry skill grows each day as you accurately log into customer details.
Strengths	Definition: Qualities (character traits like courage, creativity, empathy, etc.) or talents (e.g., engaging speaker, negotiating, problem solving) that help you do your best work. Example: Your strength in clear speaking helps you lead a quick team huddle.

💡 **Key Action:** Build your own *Glossary*, using the next two *Notes* pages, write down words and acronyms you learn in the workplace.

Notes

Notes

Afterword

One More Lap – The Full "Growing Up Corporate" Marathon Awaits

Congratulations on powering this Survival Guide. You have captured the sprint – setting SMART goals, mastering the Three P's, running with the Ten Powerful "Be's," and crossing your finish line with purpose. But **your journey does not end here.**

💡 Your Real Prize

Finishing this internship is not about a job offer. It is about the confident, capable professional you become:

- Humbled by what you have learned.
- Empowered by skills you have mastered.
- Inspired to run your next race with purpose and pride.

Run with heart, finish with excellence, and carry these lessons into every opportunity ahead.

✨ From Two Internships to a Lifelong Race

My first internship, fresh out of high school, led to real work experience, mistakes, and tough lessons in independence. Years later, a college-level internship taught me that prior jobs do not guarantee readiness. Through both experiences, mentors saw potential and invested in me, one even offered me a full-time role before my summer ended.

📖 Lessons for Every Runner

For anyone entering a workplace where you are underrepresented, especially people of color, expect to possibly work twice as hard for half the recognition. Yet each challenge you overcome cements your reputation as an analytical person and innovator.

🏙️ Dive Deeper into the Original

In **Growing Up Corporate: Let the Race Begin**, Dr. Deborah Stubblefield unfolds the full-distance race:

- Rich anecdotes from her first high-school and college internships.
- Step-by-step breakdowns of Pre-Race Prep, Get Set Go, Run & Finish Strong, and The Cool Down.
- Wisdom Moments: timeless principles to fuel both career and character.

💡 Why Read the Full Version?

While this Survival Guide gives you the core strategies and quick wins, the original book offers:

1. **Nuanced Storytelling:** Feel the highs and lows of each career-defining experience.
2. **Scripture-Infused Insights:** Thoughtful reflections that connect faith and professional growth.
3. **Comprehensive Resources:** A complete glossary, further reading, and sample cover letters – all in one place.

▓ Take Your Next Step

Use this mini guide to sprint into your first internship. Then grab the full book to:

- Plan a multi-phase internship strategy.
- Master internship performance for any type of organization.
- Build a personal brand roadmap that lasts beyond Day 1.

Whether you are mentoring a first-year student, coaching a high-potential intern, or preparing for your own corporate debut, the original **Growing Up Corporate: Let the Race Begin** is your complete playbook.

Ready for the full course? Lace up for the next lap, your corporate marathon starts now.

Get full book: **Growing Up Corporate: Let the Race Begin** (paperback) and…

The book that started it all: **Growing Up Corporate** (paperback), which highlighted her journey from intern to skill-rich professional.

Available wherever books are sold.

Acknowledgements

Thanks to my Creator and Provider, Father God – Jehovah Jireh! I acknowledge that He is the reason for every step in support of my personal and professional development. His plan was so strategic and profound.

I am also profoundly grateful to God for my family – my "Granny," parents, husband, children, and other close relatives, sister-friends, and "work siblings," who supported me along my professional journey. I also thank God for my Breakthrough Ministries family, especially our leaders and Apostles – Henry & Wilma Foster, who prayed, encouraged, and stood by me. I am forever indebted to my family (including extended and spiritual) and friends, who have all contributed to my growth and witnessed the blessings of the Lord.

About the Author

Dr. Deborah Stubblefield blends more than 20 years of corporate leadership, faith-centered mentoring, and intern-level endeavoring into a career roadmap. With an MBA, Doctorate, and four Six Sigma certifications, she has guided hundreds of individuals (e.g., interns, professionals, and leaders) who were at different phases of their professional journey. As an ordained elder, mentor, and sought-after speaker, Dr. Stubblefield lives her life daily empowering people to trust God, be intentional, and **"Grow Up Corporate"** with integrity, confidence, and a spirit of excellence.

Reaching, teaching, and inspiring people of all ages to see their greatness and fulfil their life's given purpose.

Growing Up Corporate:
Mastering the Intern Sprint Survival Guide

By Dr. Deborah Stubblefield

Our books are available at special quantity discounts for bulk purchases for sales promotions, fundraising, or educational use.

To order bulk copies for giveaways, distribution to church members or groups, sales promotions, or education, contact:

DOD Publications, LLC.
www.dodpublications.com
Wichita, Kansas 67206
Phone: (316) 202-8988